Tiana Blakely

Keto Diet for Women Over 60

Sample Keto Diet Plan for 28 days.

Mouthwatering High-Protein
And
Low-Carb Recipes.

Complete Guide to Thriving in Your Golden Years.

Dedication

This book is warmly dedicated to all women embarking on their ketogenic journey past the vibrant age of 60. Your courage to embrace change, seek health, and pursue vitality is nothing short of inspiring.

To my beloved mother, whose unwavering strength and grace continue to illuminate my path, this is for you. Your resilience and wisdom have shown me that true well-being encompasses not just the body, but the heart and spirit as well.

To every beginner, stepping into the world of keto with curiosity and hope, let this guide be your steady companion. Remember, it's never too late to transform your life, to rediscover energy, and to cultivate a profound sense of well-being.

May this journey bring you joy, health, and an abundance of moments that sparkle with clarity and contentment. Here's to embracing the golden years with gusto, to living fully, and to celebrating every step of this remarkable adventure.

Table of Contents

Introduction

Embracing a Vibrant Future

Welcome to the beginning of a transformative chapter in your life. Imagine a future where turning 60 isn't a sign of slowing down but a vibrant invitation to a healthier, more energized version of yourself. This is the promise of adopting a ketogenic lifestyle—a journey not just to weight loss but to reclaim your vitality and well-being.

You're not alone in noticing changes in your metabolism or facing the challenges of weight management as you age. It's common to feel bewildered by the myriad of health advice available, much of which overlooks the unique needs of those over 60. This guide acknowledges these struggles and offers a beacon of hope: the ketogenic diet, scientifically tailored for your specific stage of life.

The ketogenic diet isn't just another trend; it's a lifestyle shift supported by robust scientific evidence, especially beneficial for women over 60. It promises not just weight control, but also significant improvements in metabolic health, mental clarity, and a reduced risk of chronic diseases. This book is your roadmap to understanding and harnessing the power of keto, featuring easy-to-follow meal plans, delicious recipes, and practical tips for seamlessly integrating this diet into your daily life.

But this journey goes beyond the diet. It's about discovering the joy in new foods, the empowerment in taking charge of your health, and the holistic benefits that come with it—from increased physical activity and stronger social connections to a newfound zest for life.

Trust in this guide comes from its foundation in both professional expertise and personal empathy. Drawing from a wealth of scientific research and real-life success stories, it's designed to offer you not just dietary advice but a comprehensive lifestyle transformation.

As you navigate through the chapters, you'll find a blend of scientific insights, practical advice, and emotional support. Each section builds upon the last, aiming for a deep and actionable understanding of the ketogenic lifestyle.

So, with an open heart and a readiness for change, let's embark on this journey together. Turn the page, and take your first step toward a vibrant and fulfilling future. Welcome to your new chapter, where age is an asset, and vitality is a choice.

Chapter I

The Basics of the Ketogenic Diet

What Is Keto?

The ketogenic diet, known widely as "keto," is not just a modern dietary trend; its roots trace back to the early 20th century when it was meticulously crafted as a therapeutic diet for treating epilepsy. Developed in the 1920s by physicians at the Mayo Clinic, the diet was designed to mimic the beneficial effects of fasting, which had been observed to reduce the frequency and intensity of seizures in epileptic patients. By altering the body's fuel source from carbohydrates to fats, the ketogenic diet aimed to create a state of sustained ketosis, which could significantly lessen the occurrence of seizures in those affected by epilepsy, especially in cases where conventional medications were ineffective.

Over the years, the ketogenic diet has transcended its initial therapeutic purposes and has been embraced by a broader audience for its weight loss efficacy and potential health benefits. Defined by its unique macronutrient composition, the ketogenic diet is characterized by high fat, moderate protein, and very low carbohydrate intake. Specifically, the diet typically consists of approximately 70-80% fat, 15-20% protein, and only 5-10% carbohydrates. This drastic reduction in carbohydrate intake is central to the diet's mechanism, forcing the body to switch from its default energy source—glucose derived from carbohydrates—to ketones, which are metabolically generated from stored fat.

The shift to a fat-centric diet might initially seem counterintuitive, especially in a society where low-fat diets were once synonymous with health. However, the ketogenic diet challenges these norms, highlighting the body's remarkable adaptability and the multifaceted role of dietary fats. By prioritizing healthy fats and limiting carbohydrate intake, the keto diet aims to optimize weight management, improve metabolic health, and even enhance mental clarity and energy levels.

As we delve into the world of keto, it's essential to approach this eating plan with both curiosity and caution. While its benefits are manifold, particularly for those seeking a transformative approach to weight loss and health optimization, it is not without its nuances and considerations, especially for women over 60. The following chapters will guide you through understanding ketosis, navigating your nutritional needs, and implementing the ketogenic diet in a way that is not only effective but also sustainable and enjoyable, paving the way for a vibrant and healthful life.

Goals and Benefits

The ketogenic diet is more than a pathway to weight loss; it's a transformative approach to health that recalibrates the body's metabolic processes. The primary goal of adopting a ketogenic lifestyle is to shift the body's energy metabolism away from carbohydrates and towards fats. This fundamental change not only facilitates weight reduction but also ushers in a myriad of health benefits, particularly beneficial, to those who face unique health challenges as they age.

Metabolic Transformation for Weight Loss

At its core, keto aims to convert the body into a fat-burning machine. By drastically reducing carbohydrate intake, the body is forced to seek alternative energy sources, turning to stored fats for fuel. This process not only aids in effective weight management but also supports a more stable energy supply, eliminating the peaks and troughs associated with glucose-driven energy systems.

Improved Blood Sugar Control

For women over 60, maintaining blood sugar levels can become increasingly challenging due to changes in insulin sensitivity as they age. The ketogenic diet's low carbohydrate content directly contributes to stabilizing blood sugar levels, offering a potential safeguard against the development or progression of type 2 diabetes. This stable glycemic environment helps in reducing cravings and improving overall energy utilization.

Enhanced Mental Clarity

The benefits of keto extend beyond physical health, offering significant advantages for cognitive function. Ketones, produced during ketosis, are a more efficient fuel source for the brain than glucose. Many individuals report improved focus, clearer thinking, and enhanced memory function under ketosis. For aging women, these cognitive benefits are particularly valuable in maintaining mental acuity and potentially mitigating the risk of cognitive decline.

Reduced Inflammation

Chronic inflammation is a common concern as the body ages, contributing to various health issues, from arthritis to heart disease. The ketogenic diet has been shown to reduce inflammation, thanks to the anti-inflammatory properties of ketones and the elimination of sugar and certain processed foods known to drive inflammatory responses. This reduction in inflammation can lead to decreased pain and increased mobility, significantly improving quality of life.

Potential Reduction in the Risk of Chronic Diseases

Adopting a ketogenic lifestyle may also offer protective benefits against various chronic diseases. By improving markers of metabolic health, such as blood pressure, cholesterol levels, and blood sugar control, the risk of heart disease, stroke, and diabetes can be significantly reduced. Furthermore, preliminary research suggests a potential link between ketosis and a lower risk of certain cancers and neurological disorders, although more research is needed in these areas.

In essence, the ketogenic diet opens the door to a multitude of health benefits, particularly for women over 60, who may be navigating the complexities of aging. By embracing keto, not only can weight management become more attainable, but the journey towards a healthier, more vibrant life becomes clearer.

The Metabolic Shift

At the heart of the ketogenic diet is a profound metabolic process known as ketosis, a state where the body, in the absence of sufficient glucose, turns to stored fat as its primary source of energy. This shift from glucose to fat metabolism is not just the cornerstone of the ketogenic diet's efficacy but also a gateway to numerous health benefits. Understanding ketosis is crucial for anyone embarking on a ketogenic lifestyle, and looking to optimize their health and vitality.

Understanding Metabolic Shifts

With age, the body's metabolism naturally slows down, a change attributed to a decrease in muscle mass and hormonal adjustments. This slowdown affects how the body processes foods, necessitating adjustments in caloric intake and nutritional balance to prevent weight gain and support overall health.

Adapting Dietary Needs: To accommodate these metabolic changes, women over 60 may need to reduce their caloric intake slightly while ensuring they still receive the necessary nutrients for optimal health. Increasing protein intake can help mitigate muscle loss (sarcopenia) while focusing on nutrient-dense foods can support a slower metabolism.

Essential Nutrients and Vitamins

Protein for Muscle Maintenance: Adequate protein intake is vital for preserving muscle mass and strength. Sources such as lean meats, fish, dairy, and legumes should be integral parts of the diet.

Calcium and Vitamin D for Bone Health: To combat the risk of osteoporosis, sufficient calcium and vitamin D are crucial. While sunlight is a natural source of vitamin D, foods like fatty fish, egg yolks, and fortified foods, along with calcium-rich foods like dairy products, leafy greens, and almonds, should be included in the diet.

B Vitamins for Energy and Brain Health: B vitamins, particularly B12, are essential for energy production and maintaining proper brain function. Older adults may have a harder time absorbing vitamin B12, making fortified foods or supplements necessary.

Fiber for Digestive Health: A high-fiber diet supports digestive health and can help manage blood sugar levels. Vegetables, fruits, nuts, seeds, and whole grains are excellent fiber sources.

Omega-3 Fatty Acids for Heart Health: Omega-3s, found in fatty fish, flaxseeds, and walnuts, are essential for maintaining heart health and reducing inflammation.

Hydration and Bone Health

The Role of Hydration: Adequate hydration is vital for overall health, aiding in digestion, nutrient absorption, and cellular function. As the sense of thirst may diminish with age, it's important to consciously include fluids throughout the day, prioritizing water and other low-calorie, non-caffeinated beverages.

Water

It is necessary to drink enough clean water.

25 ml \ 0,85 oz of fluid per kilogram of weight daily.

Supporting Bone Health: Beyond calcium and vitamin D, magnesium and vitamin K are also important for bone health. Green leafy vegetables, nuts, seeds, and whole grains can provide these nutrients. Regular weight-bearing and strength-training exercises further support bone density and overall skeletal health.

In conclusion, addressing the nutritional needs of women over 60 requires a holistic approach that accommodates changes in metabolism, emphasizes essential nutrients and vitamins, and recognizes the critical importance of hydration and bone health. By focusing on a balanced, nutrient-dense diet and staying active, women can significantly enhance their health and well-being during these years, laying a strong foundation for a vibrant and fulfilling life.

The Transition to Ketosis

Under normal dietary conditions, the body relies on glucose, derived from carbohydrate consumption, as its main energy source. Glucose fuels everything from brain function to muscle activity. However, when carbohydrate intake is drastically reduced, the body's glucose reserves become insufficient to meet its energy demands. This shortage triggers the liver to start converting fat, both from the diet and the body's stores, into fatty acids and ketone bodies. Ketone bodies, particularly beta-hydroxybutyrate, acetoacetate, and acetone, then become the main energy source, effectively replacing glucose. This metabolic adaptation to ketosis is a natural response, reminiscent of the body's survival mechanism during times of fasting or food scarcity.

Achieving Ketosis through Dietary Changes

The journey to ketosis begins with significant dietary adjustments, primarily the reduction of carbohydrate intake to about 20 to 50 grams per day, depending on individual metabolism and activity level. This drastic reduction is crucial as it lowers blood sugar and insulin levels, paving the way for the body to enter ketosis. Foods high in carbohydrates, such as grains, sugar, fruits, and starchy vegetables, are replaced with high-fat and moderate-protein foods to ensure that the body has the necessary ingredients to make the metabolic switch.

Understanding the Signs of Ketosis

Entering ketosis is a unique experience, with several signs indicating the body's transition. These include increased energy and mental clarity, reduced appetite, and a distinct change in breath odor or a metallic taste in the mouth, known as "keto breath." It's also common to experience initial side effects, often referred to as the "keto flu," which may include fatigue, headaches, and dizziness as the body adjusts to its new fuel source. These symptoms typically subside as the body becomes keto-adapted.

Monitoring Ketosis

For those embarking on the ketogenic diet, monitoring ketone levels can provide valuable feedback on whether the body has entered ketosis. This can be done through urine strips, blood ketone meters, or breath analyzers, each measuring different types of ketones. While monitoring isn't essential for everyone, it can offer insights and motivation, especially in the early stages of the diet.

The metabolic shift to ketosis is a central element of the ketogenic diet's success, which may benefit greatly from this shift in energy metabolism. By understanding and embracing the process of ketosis, individuals can more effectively tailor their diet to achieve optimal health outcomes, leveraging the body's innate ability to burn fat for fuel.

Signs and Symptoms of Ketosis

As individuals embark on the ketogenic journey, especially women over 60 seeking to enhance their health and vitality, recognizing the signs and symptoms of ketosis can be both reassuring and motivating. Ketosis, a metabolic state where the body efficiently burns fat for energy, manifests through several notable indicators. Understanding these signs helps in navigating the diet more effectively and ensures that one is on the right path to achieving their health goals.

Increased Energy and Mental Clarity

One of the most welcomed signs of ketosis is a significant boost in energy levels and mental clarity. As the body transitions from relying on glucose to ketones for energy, many report feeling more alert, focused, and energetic throughout the day. This increase in cognitive function and physical stamina is particularly beneficial for women over 60, as it can improve overall quality of life and engagement in daily activities.

Reduced Appetite and Cravings

Another hallmark of ketosis is a noticeable reduction in appetite and cravings. Ketones have a more stable energy output than glucose, which helps regulate the body's hunger signals. Many find that the constant hunger and cravings associated with high-carbohydrate diets diminish or disappear entirely, making it easier to stick to the ketogenic plan and potentially leading to a more mindful relationship with food.

Weight Loss

Weight loss is often the primary goal for many adopting the ketogenic diet, and it's also a clear indicator of ketosis. As the body becomes adept at burning fat for fuel, stored fat is reduced, leading to weight loss. This can be particularly encouraging for older women, for whom weight loss might be more challenging due to metabolic changes associated with aging.

Temporary Side Effects: The Keto Flu

While the transition to ketosis offers many positive signs, it can also bring about temporary side effects, commonly referred to as the "keto flu." This term describes a collection of symptoms, including fatigue, headaches, nausea, dizziness, and irritability, that some experience in the first few days to weeks of starting the diet. These symptoms are a result of the body adapting to its new energy source and usually resolve once the body becomes keto-adapted. Staying hydrated and replenishing electrolytes can help alleviate these symptoms.

Other Physical Indicators

There are also physical signs that can indicate the body has entered ketosis, such as a fruity or metallic taste in the mouth, known as "keto breath," and changes in urination frequency. Some may also notice a temporary increase in thirst or dry mouth, signaling the body's need for more fluids during this metabolic shift.

Recognizing the signs and symptoms of ketosis can empower women over 60 with the knowledge that their bodies are adapting to a more efficient energy source. These indicators not only serve as milestones on the ketogenic journey but also highlight the body's remarkable ability to transform and thrive on this health-optimizing path.

The Importance of Fat, Protein, and Carbs

In the context of ketosis and overall health, the balance of macronutrients—fat, protein, and carbohydrates—plays a pivotal role. Fats, the primary energy source on a ketogenic diet, should come from healthy, unprocessed sources like avocados, nuts, seeds, and olive oil, providing essential fatty acids and fat-soluble vitamins. Protein supports muscle health and overall bodily functions without knocking the body out of ketosis, making it important to consume adequate but not excessive amounts. Carbohydrates, while significantly reduced, should primarily come from nutrient-dense, fibrous vegetables, and low-glycemic fruits, ensuring that the body receives vital nutrients without disrupting ketosis.

For older adults exploring the ketogenic diet, these health implications underscore the potential for not just a healthier diet but a healthier lifestyle. The benefits of ketosis extend beyond simple weight loss, offering a pathway to preserved muscle mass, enhanced brain function, and improved metabolic health, contributing to a more vibrant, active, and fulfilling life in the later years.

Fat: The Primary Energy Source

In the ketogenic diet, fat takes center stage, not as the villain in our dietary story, but as the hero. Long-standing myths have painted dietary fat as the main culprit behind heart disease and weight gain. However, modern research and the foundational principles of the ketogenic diet challenge these misconceptions, highlighting the essential role of healthy fats in maintaining overall well-being.

Healthy fats, such as those found in avocados, nuts, seeds, olive oil, and fatty fish, are crucial for the ketogenic diet. They provide the majority of daily caloric intake, replacing carbohydrates as the primary energy source. This shift encourages the body to burn fat for fuel, leading to weight loss and improved metabolic efficiency. Moreover, these fats contribute to satiety, helping to curb hunger longer than carbohydrates, making it easier to maintain a calorie deficit without feeling deprived.

Beyond energy, fats play a vital role in nutrient absorption. Fat-soluble vitamins A, D, E, and K require dietary fat for their absorption and utilization within the body. These vitamins are crucial for various bodily functions, including bone health, blood clotting, and immune system performance. By ensuring adequate intake of healthy fats, the ketogenic diet supports the absorption of these essential nutrients, contributing to overall health.

Protein: Essential for Muscle and Repair

While fat is the primary energy source in the ketogenic diet, protein plays a critical role in maintaining muscle mass and supporting bodily repair, especially crucial for aging bodies. As we age, preserving muscle mass becomes a key concern due to its role in metabolism, strength, and overall functionality.

Protein intake on the ketogenic diet should be moderate. This balance is essential to prevent the body from converting excess protein into glucose through gluconeogenesis, which could potentially interrupt the state of ketosis. The goal is to consume just enough protein to support muscle maintenance and repair without undermining the metabolic state central to the diet's effectiveness.

Complete Proteins - include the full spectrum of amino acids essential to the body. Animal Proteins: Fish, Eggs, Dairy products, Red meat, Poultry

Incomplete Proteins - lack one or more amino acids, or they are present in very small quantities. Plant Proteins: Tofu, tempeh, edamame, Lentils, Chickpeas, Nuts, Spirulina, Quinoa, Mycoprotein, Seeds, Dark-colored, leafy greens and vegetables, Seitan

Carbohydrates: Minimizing Intake

The cornerstone of the ketogenic diet lies in significantly reducing carbohydrate intake, a necessary step to enter and maintain the state of ketosis where the body optimally burns fat for energy. Understanding which carbohydrates to limit or eliminate is key to navigating this diet successfully, especially for individuals aiming to transform their health and lifestyle.

Limiting Carbohydrate Intake

To achieve ketosis, it's essential to limit daily carbohydrate intake to about 20-50 grams. This restriction primarily targets high-carb foods such as sugars, grains (including wheat, oats, and rice), starchy vegetables (like potatoes and corn), and most fruits, which can quickly exceed the daily carb limit. Instead, the focus shifts towards foods that support ketosis without spiking blood sugar levels.

The Role of Fiber-Rich Vegetables

While minimizing carb intake, incorporating fiber-rich, low-carb vegetables into your diet is crucial for maintaining overall health. Vegetables like leafy greens (spinach, kale), cruciferous veggies (broccoli, cauliflower), and others like zucchini and bell peppers are not only low in net carbs (total carbs minus fiber) but also rich in vitamins, minerals, and fiber. Fiber plays a vital role in digestive health, helping to prevent constipation and promote gut health, which can be a concern when significantly reducing carbohydrate intake.

Nutritional Balance and Health

These fiber-rich, low-carb vegetables also contribute to the nutritional balance of the ketogenic diet. They provide essential nutrients that might be lacking when high-carb foods are eliminated. For example, leafy greens are an excellent source of vitamin K, magnesium, and calcium, while avocados offer healthy fats along with vitamin E and potassium. This emphasis on nutrient-dense, low-carb vegetables ensures that the body receives a wide range of vital nutrients for optimal health, supporting everything from bone health to immune system function.

Optimal Meal Portions for Weight Management

The recommended amount of grams to consume per meal can vary widely depending on individual dietary needs, goals, and the specific diet plan you're following. However, for general guidance, the Harvard T.H. Chan School of Public Health provides a useful framework for building a healthy plate that focuses on the quality of nutrients rather than strict gram amounts. This approach emphasizes the importance of incorporating various foods in appropriate proportions to meet nutritional needs.

In the context of calorie-controlled diets, including those aimed at weight loss, portion control is crucial. An average meal might range from 400 to 500 grams in total weight, combining all components like proteins, vegetables, fats, and minimal carbs, especially if following a low-carb or ketogenic diet. This range ensures a balanced intake that supports metabolic health and satiety without excess calories.

For specific dietary programs, such as ketogenic diets, the macronutrient distribution is critical. A typical keto meal might consist of about 70-75% calories from fat, 20-25% from protein, and 5-10% from carbohydrates. Translating this into grams will depend on the total caloric intake. For example, in a 500-calorie meal, this could equate to roughly 39-42 grams of fat, 25-31 grams of protein, and 5-12 grams of carbs.

It's important to personalize your diet based on your energy needs, which are influenced by factors like age, gender, weight, height, and physical activity level. Tools such as the Dietary Guidelines for Americans provide equations and recommendations for estimating individual caloric needs and can serve as a basis for calculating gram amounts per meal tailored to personal goals.

For precise nutritional planning and to ensure you're meeting your specific dietary requirements, consulting with a registered dietitian or a healthcare provider is recommended. They can provide tailored advice based on your health status, dietary preferences, and weight management goals.

Implementing the Keto Diet

Successfully implementing the ketogenic diet involves careful planning and mindful eating. Begin by assessing your current diet, and identifying high-carb foods to replace with keto-friendly alternatives. Planning meals around protein sources and healthy fats, complemented by low-carb vegetables, is a practical approach to ensure you stay within your carb limit while still enjoying a varied and nutritious diet.

For those new to the ketogenic lifestyle, starting slowly and making gradual adjustments can make the transition easier and more sustainable. Keeping track of carb intake through a food diary or a mobile app can also help you stay on track and make informed choices about your meals.

In summary, minimizing carbohydrate intake is crucial for maintaining ketosis, but ensuring the carbs you consume come from nutrient-rich, fiber-dense sources is equally important. By focusing on low-carb vegetables and carefully planning your meals, you can enjoy the health benefits of the ketogenic diet while supporting your body's nutritional needs and digestive health.

High-quality protein sources include grass-fed meat, poultry, fish, eggs, and some dairy products like Greek yogurt and cheese. Plant-based proteins such as legumes, nuts, and seeds are also beneficial, though they should be consumed in moderation due to their carb content.

For older adults, especially women over 60 embarking on a ketogenic lifestyle, paying attention to protein intake is crucial. It ensures the body receives enough amino acids for muscle repair and maintenance while continuing to burn fat for energy. This careful balance supports not only the preservation of muscle mass but also overall bodily functions, ensuring that the ketogenic diet is both effective and sustainable in the long term.

Getting Started

Educate Yourself

Embarking on the ketogenic journey begins with a solid foundation of knowledge. Understand the principles of ketosis, where your body switches from using glucose to fat as its primary energy source. This metabolic state is achieved by significantly reducing carbohydrate intake while increasing fat consumption. Familiarize yourself with the health benefits, potential side effects, and the scientific rationale behind fat adaptation. Resources can include medical journals, reputable keto-focused websites, and books by leading ketogenic diet researchers.

Clean Out Your Pantry

Preparing your environment is as crucial as preparing your mind. Begin with a thorough audit of your kitchen. Eliminate foods that are high in carbohydrates, such as bread, pasta, sugary snacks, and cereals, and replace them with keto-friendly alternatives like nuts, seeds, avocados, and low-carb vegetables. This step prevents temptation and makes choosing healthy options easier.

Go Grocery Shopping

Arm yourself with a keto-friendly shopping list to restock your pantry and refrigerator. Prioritize whole, unprocessed foods like grass-fed meats, fatty fish, eggs, high-quality oils, and a colorful array of vegetables that are low in carbs but high in fiber and nutrients. Organic and grass-fed options are preferable for their higher nutrient profiles and absence of antibiotics and hormones.

Buy a Scale

A kitchen scale allows you to measure your ingredients and meal portions with precision, removing the guesswork from your diet. This is especially crucial in a keto diet, where the ratio of fats, proteins, and carbs can significantly influence your results. By accurately weighing your food, you can track your intake more effectively, make necessary adjustments with ease, and stay on course toward achieving your dietary objectives.

Additionally, investing in a weight scale is equally important. A weight scale will enable you to monitor your body weight changes regularly, providing insight into how well your body is responding to the diet. Together, these tools are invaluable for anyone serious about starting and successfully maintaining a keto diet, as they offer the precision and accountability needed to achieve your health and fitness goals.

Plan Your Meals

Successful adherence to the keto diet often hinges on planning. Draft a meal plan that suits your lifestyle, preferences, and nutritional needs, ensuring it fits within your daily macro limits. Consider preparing meals in advance to save time and prevent decision fatigue. Utilizing online meal planners and keto recipes can inspire variety and excitement in your diet.

Track Your Macros

Keeping a close eye on your intake of fats, proteins, and carbohydrates is essential for maintaining ketosis. Use a food tracking app or journal to record everything you eat, ensuring you stay within your macro limits. This habit helps in making informed adjustments to your diet as needed.

Stay Hydrated and Mind Your Electrolytes

The ketogenic diet can lead to increased water and electrolyte loss, especially in the early stages. Drink ample water and consume foods rich in potassium (avocado, nuts), magnesium (leafy greens, fish), and sodium (salt in your foods) to maintain electrolyte balance. Consider supplements if necessary.

Listen to Your Body

Each person's experience with keto is unique. Pay attention to how you feel, both physically and mentally. If you encounter persistent fatigue, irritability, or other adverse symptoms, reassess your diet to ensure it's balanced and consult with a healthcare professional to make necessary adjustments.

Seek Support

A strong support system can greatly enhance your keto journey. Connect with others following the ketogenic lifestyle through online communities, local groups, or friends and family. Sharing experiences, challenges, and successes can provide motivation, accountability, and valuable insights.

Adjusting to Keto Life

Managing Social Situations

Social gatherings can pose challenges to maintaining your keto lifestyle. Plan ahead by reviewing restaurant menus online, bringing your keto-friendly dishes to share at parties, or suggesting gatherings that don't revolve around food. Communication is key; don't hesitate to discuss your dietary needs with friends and family.

Dealing with Cravings

Cravings for carbs and sugar are common, especially in the initial stages of the diet. Arm yourself with keto-friendly snacks and desserts to satiate these cravings without derailing your progress. Understanding that these cravings diminish over time as your body fully adapts to ketosis can also be comforting.

Acknowledging the Adaptation Period

The transition to ketosis can be accompanied by temporary discomforts, often referred to as the "keto flu." Symptoms like headaches, fatigue, and irritability are normal and temporary. Staying hydrated, properly managing electrolytes, and gradually reducing carb intake (instead of an abrupt cut) can ease this transition.

Staying Flexible and Patient

Flexibility and patience are virtues in the keto journey. Recognize that adaptation takes time and that minor setbacks do not equate to failure. Be willing to experiment with your diet to find what best suits your body and lifestyle.

Persistence Pays Off

Consistency is key to realizing the full benefits of the ketogenic diet. While the initial adaptation period can be challenging, staying the course can lead to significant improvements in weight, energy levels, and overall health.

Long-Term Considerations

Incorporating Variety and Balance

To ensure nutritional adequacy and prevent boredom, incorporate a wide variety of foods within your keto framework. Experiment with new recipes, try different keto-friendly vegetables and vary your protein sources to keep meals interesting and balanced.

Making Adjustments for Personal Health

Individual health goals and conditions may necessitate adjustments to the standard keto diet. For instance, athletes may require more protein.

The ketogenic diet holds a remarkable potential to transform health and well-being. By aligning dietary habits with the body's natural processes for energy production and fat utilization, this lifestyle offers a pathway to not just manage weight, but to enhance overall vitality, cognitive function, and metabolic health. The journey into ketogenic living is not merely about subtracting carbohydrates but about enriching your life with nutritious foods that nourish and sustain your body's needs.

As you consider embarking on this transformative journey, approach the ketogenic lifestyle with curiosity and openness. The initial steps into ketosis represent an opportunity to rediscover food as a source of both pleasure and health, explore new tastes, and embrace the positive changes that come with mindfully nurturing your body. It's a chance to challenge old myths about dietary fats, to learn the intricacies of your body's metabolic processes, and to witness firsthand the profound effects of dietary change on your physical and mental well-being.

Commitment to this lifestyle change means embracing a new perspective on health—one that values balance, listens to the body's signals and recognizes the importance of adaptability. The ketogenic diet is not a one-size-fits-all solution but a flexible framework that can be tailored to meet your unique needs and goals, especially as they evolve with age.

Remember, the journey to keto-adaptation is as much about the mind as it is about the body. Patience and persistence are your allies, guiding you through the adaptation period and beyond. Challenges along the way are not setbacks but opportunities to learn more about your body and how it responds to different foods and macronutrient balances.

To those of you stepping into the world of ketogenic living, know that you're embarking on a deeply rewarding path. The benefits extend far beyond the scale, offering a renewed sense of energy, clarity, and health that can profoundly impact your quality of life. So, take this journey one step at a time, with a spirit of adventure and a commitment to your health. The potential for transformation is immense, and it all starts with the decision to make a change. Welcome to the ketogenic lifestyle, where your journey to wellness is just beginning.

Chapter II

Keto Diet Essentials: Foods to Embrace and Avoid

Embarking on a ketogenic journey means prioritizing foods that support a state of ketosis while providing essential nutrients for aging gracefully. This section outlines the key foods to include in your diet and those to avoid, ensuring a rich, varied, and healthful dietary experience.

Foods to Include

Protein:

When following a ketogenic diet, prioritizing high-quality, minimally processed protein sources is essential for overall health and well-being. These protein sources not only support muscle maintenance and growth but also provide vital nutrients that are crucial for optimal body function. Here's a closer look at each recommended protein type:

Free-Range Poultry: Chickens and turkeys that have been raised with access to the outdoors tend to have a higher quality of life and can provide meat that is richer in omega-3 fatty acids compared to conventionally raised poultry. Look for labels like "free-range," "pasture-raised," or "organic" to ensure you're getting the best quality. This includes chicken, turkey, and potentially other poultry like duck.

Wild-Caught Fish: Fish that are caught in their natural habitats are generally lower in pollutants and higher in omega-3 fatty acids than their farmed counterparts. Salmon, mackerel, sardines, and trout are excellent choices. These omega-3s are crucial for heart health, brain function, and reducing inflammation in the body.

Grass-Fed Meats: Beef, lamb, and other meats from animals that have been fed a natural grass diet, rather than grain, contain more omega-3 fatty acids, conjugated linoleic acid (CLA), and antioxidants such as vitamin E. Grass-fed meats are often leaner and carry a different flavor profile compared to grain-fed meats.

Eggs: Eggs are a powerhouse of nutrition, providing high-quality protein, healthy fats, vitamins, and minerals. Opt for eggs from free-range or pastured hens, as they tend to have a higher content of omega-3 fatty acids and vitamin E.

Wild-Caught Seafood: Beyond fish, other seafood like shrimp, crab, and lobster, when wild-caught, are excellent sources of protein and important nutrients like iodine and zinc. They offer variety and richness to a ketogenic diet, allowing for creative and delicious meal planning.

Incorporating these high-quality protein sources into your diet supports the goals of the ketogenic lifestyle by providing essential nutrients and fats that align with ketosis. Additionally, choosing minimally processed and ethically sourced options helps reduce the intake of added hormones, antibiotics, and toxins, further promoting your health and the environment.

Fats and Oils:

On a ketogenic diet, your main energy sources should come from fats that not only help you stay in ketosis but also support overall health, particularly heart and brain function. Here's how to ensure you're getting the right types of fats:

Omega-3 Fatty Acids: Essential for brain health and reducing inflammation, omega-3s can be found abundantly in seafood. Opt for fatty fish like salmon, mackerel, and sardines, as well as shellfish. If fish isn't a regular part of your diet, consider supplements such as fish oil or krill oil to get your omega-3s.

Monounsaturated Fats: These heart-healthy fats are vital for maintaining good cholesterol levels and providing energy. Avocados are a fantastic source, alongside olives and their oils. Egg yolks and high-quality, grass-fed butter also provide these beneficial fats.

Saturated Fats: While often maligned in the past, certain saturated fats can be part of a healthy keto diet. Coconut oil is a prime example, known for its medium-chain triglycerides (MCTs) that the body can easily convert into ketones. Ghee (clarified butter) and butter from grass-fed cows are also excellent choices, as are non-hydrogenated animal fats like beef tallow and lard. Remember to choose these from high-quality, responsibly raised sources to avoid added hormones and antibiotics.

Polyunsaturated Fats from Natural Sources: While not a primary focus, these fats are also part of a balanced keto diet. Duck and chicken fat, when sourced from well-raised animals, can provide a mix of beneficial fats including some omega-6 fatty acids, which are essential in moderation.

Including a variety of these fats in your diet can help ensure you're getting a wide range of nutrients while following a ketogenic lifestyle. Always prioritize quality and consider how each fat source fits into your overall health goals.

Fresh Vegetables:

For those following a ketogenic lifestyle, prioritizing low-carb vegetables is crucial for maintaining ketosis while ensuring nutrient intake. Emphasize organic, pesticide-free produce whenever possible to reduce exposure to harmful chemicals. Here's a guide to the vegetables best suited for a keto diet, focusing on leafy greens and non-starchy options to keep your carbohydrate intake minimal. You can enjoy sweeter vegetables like tomatoes and peppers but do so sparingly due to their higher sugar content.

Leafy Greens & Cruciferous Vegetables: These are your go-to for vitamins, minerals, and fiber.

Spinach, Kale, Collard Greens, Swiss Chard, Beet Greens, Dandelion Greens.

Broccoli, Cauliflower, Cabbage, Brussels Sprouts.

Root Vegetables & Bulbs (Moderate Intake Recommended): Some root vegetables are higher in carbs but can be included in small amounts.

Onions, Garlic, Shallots, Leeks, Turnips, Radishes, Celery Root.

Fermented Vegetables: Great for gut health.

Sauerkraut, Kimchi (watch for added sugars), Dill Pickles (opt for varieties without added sugar).

Sprouts & Microgreens: Nutrient-dense and low in carbs.

Alfalfa Sprouts, Bean Sprouts, Microgreen Varieties.

Other Non-Starchy Vegetables: These can be eaten more freely.

Celery, Cucumbers, Mushrooms, Asparagus, Bamboo Shoots, Olives, Snow Peas (in moderation).

Salad Greens & Lettuces: Perfect for bulk and fiber with minimal carbs.

Romaine, Arugula, Boston Lettuce, Endive, Escarole, Fennel, Mache, Sorrel, Radicchio, Chicory.

Including a variety of these vegetables in your meals will not only help keep your carb intake in check but also provide a rich source of vitamins, minerals, and fiber essential for optimal health. Remember, moderation is key for vegetables that are slightly higher in carbs.

Dairy Products:

Incorporating dairy into a ketogenic diet can add both flavor and nutritional value, especially when choosing products that align with keto principles. Focus on full-fat, raw, or organic dairy options to maximize the health benefits while minimizing exposure to unnecessary additives and hormones. Dairy can be a good source of fats, probiotics, and essential nutrients, but it's important to be mindful of carbohydrate content. Here's a refined approach to including dairy in your keto diet:

High-Fat Cheeses: Look for varieties that are both rich in flavor and fat content. Options include:

Mascarpone: A creamy cheese perfect for adding richness to recipes.

Soft and Hard Cheeses: These can vary widely, from brie to cheddar, offering a range of flavors and textures.

Cream Cheese: Ideal for adding creaminess to dishes or as a spread.

Creams & Cultured Dairy: Heavy Whipping Cream: A staple for adding fat to coffee, desserts, or savory dishes.

Full-fat sour Cream: Choose versions without additives for a clean keto option. It's great as a topping or ingredient in recipes.

Full-Fat Cottage Cheese: Offers a good source of protein and fat, but be mindful of portion sizes due to varying carb content.

Unsweetened Whole Milk Yogurt: Although a bit higher in carbs, it's beneficial for its probiotics. Limit intake and choose unsweetened varieties to stay within your carb limit.

When selecting dairy products, always opt for those without added sugars, starches, or unnecessary additives to stay true to your ketogenic goals. Dairy products not only provide a delicious source of fat but can also enhance the overall nutritional quality of your diet. However, monitoring portion sizes and carb content is key to maintaining ketosis and achieving your health objectives.

Nuts and Seeds:

Nuts are a wonderful addition to the ketogenic diet due to their low carbohydrate content and high levels of healthy fats. They're not just great for snacking; nuts like almonds, macadamias, and walnuts can also be transformed into nut flours, providing a fantastic alternative to traditional flour in baking. This allows for more flexibility in creating keto-friendly treats without compromising your dietary goals. Here's a closer look at how these nuts fit into a ketogenic lifestyle:

Almonds: Almonds are incredibly versatile. They can be eaten whole as a snack, sliced or chopped into salads, or ground into almond flour for baking. Almond flour is particularly popular in keto recipes for bread, pancakes, and other baked goods due to its low-carb content and pleasant taste.

Macadamias: Known for their rich, buttery flavor, macadamias are among the highest in fats and lowest in carbs, making them an excellent keto snack. Macadamia nuts can also be ground into flour or used to make a dairy-free milk alternative that's keto-friendly.

Walnuts: Walnuts are not only low in carbs but also high in omega-3 fatty acids, which are beneficial for heart health. They add a wonderful texture and nutty flavor to salads, baked goods, and snack mixes. A walnut meal can also be used in baking, although it's less common than almond flour.

Using nut flour in your baking provides a nutrient-dense alternative to traditional flour, helping to keep your carbohydrate intake low while increasing your intake of healthy fats and proteins. Additionally, these nuts contain essential vitamins and minerals, adding nutritional value to your keto diet. Remember to monitor portion sizes, as nuts are calorie-dense, and excessive consumption could hinder weight management goals.

Beverages:

Hydration is a vital component of the ketogenic diet, helping to support metabolism, energy levels, and overall health. While water should be your primary source of hydration, several other keto-friendly options can keep hydration interesting and enjoyable. Here's a guide to staying hydrated on a keto diet, including a variety of beverages that fit within the guidelines:

Water: The most essential drink for staying hydrated. It's calorie-free, and carb-free, and helps to flush toxins from your body. To enhance the flavor, consider adding slices of keto-friendly fruits like lemon or lime, but remember to limit your intake due to their natural sugars.

Herbal Tea: Herbal teas are a great way to stay hydrated without caffeine. Options like peppermint, chamomile, and hibiscus can offer a soothing, flavorful alternative to plain water. Since they're naturally free of calories and carbs, you can enjoy them throughout the day.

Bulletproof Coffee: A staple for many on the ketogenic diet, bulletproof coffee combines coffee with grass-fed butter and MCT oil or coconut oil. This concoction not only helps you stay hydrated but also boosts energy levels and provides a good dose of healthy fats to keep you in ketosis.

Decaf Tea and Decaf Coffee: For those who enjoy tea and coffee without caffeine, decaffeinated options are keto-friendly and can be enjoyed any time of day. Just be sure to avoid adding sugar; opt for a natural, low-carb sweetener if needed.

Flavored Seltzer Water: A refreshing option that can satisfy your craving for something carbonated without the sugar and carbs found in traditional sodas. Look for varieties without added sugars or artificial sweeteners.

Unsweetened Almond Milk and Coconut Milk: These milk alternatives are low in carbs and calories, making them great options for staying hydrated. They can also be used in keto recipes or enjoyed on their own. Opt for the unsweetened versions to avoid added sugars.

Lemon and Lime Juice: Adding a splash of lemon or lime juice to water can enhance its flavor and provide vitamin C. However, because fruits contain natural sugars, it's important to use these juices sparingly to avoid excess carb intake.

Staying well-hydrated is key to feeling your best on a ketogenic diet. By incorporating a variety of these beverages into your daily routine, you can ensure adequate hydration while enjoying a range of flavors that keep your taste buds satisfied.

Sweeteners:

For those following a ketogenic diet, managing sweet cravings without disrupting ketosis is crucial. Natural, low-carb sweeteners are the key to enjoying sweet flavors while maintaining stable blood sugar levels. These sweeteners provide the taste of sugar without the high carb content, making them ideal for keto-friendly cooking and baking. Here's a closer look at each option:

Erythritol: A sugar alcohol with almost no calories and a glycemic index of zero, erythritol doesn't spike blood sugar or insulin levels, making it a popular choice for keto desserts and beverages.

Splenda Liquid (not "Splendor-liquid"): This is a no-calorie version of Splenda specifically designed to not impact blood sugar, making it suitable for adding to drinks or recipes where a liquid sweetener is preferred.

Inulin and Chicory Root: Extracted from chicory root, inulin is a type of prebiotic fiber that can sweeten foods while promoting digestive health. It has a minimal impact on blood sugar levels.

Lo Han Guo (Monk Fruit): Derived from the monk fruit, Lo Han Guo is a natural sweetener that contains zero calories and has no impact on blood sugar, making it perfect for keto dieters.

Liquid Stevia: Stevia is a natural sweetener derived from the leaves of the Stevia plant. The liquid form is particularly versatile for sweetening beverages and recipes without adding carbs.

Xylitol: Another sugar alcohol, xylitol is lower in calories than sugar and has a low glycemic index. However, it's slightly higher in carbs than erythritol, so it should be used sparingly. Note: Xylitol is toxic to dogs, so be careful if you have pets.

Swerve: A blend of erythritol, oligosaccharides, and natural flavors, Swerve is a zero-calorie sweetener that measures cup-for-cup like sugar, making it easy to use in recipes.

These sweeteners can be used in a variety of ways, from sweetening your morning coffee to creating indulgent, keto-friendly desserts. When incorporating them into your diet, it's important to consider personal taste preferences and possible digestive sensitivities, as some individuals may experience discomfort with certain sugar alcohols. By carefully selecting and using these sweeteners, you can satisfy your sweet tooth without compromising your ketogenic lifestyle.

Spices:

Spices are invaluable allies in the ketogenic kitchen, offering a way to infuse your meals with deep, complex flavors without the addition of unwanted carbs. Most spices and herbs are naturally low in carbohydrates, making them perfect for enhancing your dishes while keeping within the guidelines of a keto diet. Here's how you can utilize a selection of spices and herbs to elevate your cooking:

Sea Salt: An essential seasoning that enhances the natural flavors of your ingredients. Unlike processed table salt, sea salt contains trace minerals.

Peppermint: Fresh or dried, peppermint adds a refreshing note to teas, salads, and certain keto-friendly desserts.

Ginger: Fresh or powdered, ginger brings warmth and zing to dishes. It's great in marinades, stir-fries, and tea.

Basil: This aromatic herb can transform simple dishes into gourmet meals. Fresh basil leaves are perfect in salads, over-grilled meats, or in keto-friendly pesto.

Chili Pepper: Fresh, dried, or powdered, chili peppers add heat and depth to dishes, from soups and stews to meats.

Cloves: Ground cloves have a warm, sweet, and slightly bitter flavor, ideal for spiced keto desserts and some savory dishes.

Thyme: Its earthy flavor complements a wide range of foods, from roasted vegetables to meats and soups.

Cilantro or Coriander Seeds: Fresh cilantro leaves brighten up any dish, while coriander seeds are great in spice mixes and curries.

Rosemary: With its piney aroma, rosemary is perfect for seasoning meats, especially lamb, pork, and chicken.

Black Pepper: Freshly ground black pepper adds a spicy kick to virtually any dish, enhancing flavor instantly.

Cumin Seeds: Ground or whole, cumin adds a warm, earthy note to spice mixes, soups, and meat dishes.

Oregano: This robust herb is a staple in Italian and Mediterranean cooking, perfect for seasoning meats, sauces, and vegetables.

Turmeric: Known for its vibrant color and health benefits, turmeric adds a warm, bitter flavor to curries, soups, and rice dishes.

Cayenne Pepper: A pinch can add significant heat and a metabolism-boosting effect to your meals.

Cinnamon: Sweet and warming, cinnamon is perfect for keto-friendly desserts or even adding a unique twist to savory dishes.

Mustard Seeds: Used in pickling, marinades, and sauces, mustard seeds add a spicy, tangy flavor to dishes.

Parsley: Fresh parsley is versatile, adding a light, fresh flavor to salads, soups, and garnishes.

Dill: Fresh or dried, dill is excellent with fish, yogurt sauces, and salads.

Sage: With its strong aromatic flavor, sage is ideal for seasoning poultry, pork, and sausages.

Incorporating a variety of these spices and herbs into your ketogenic diet not only maximizes flavor but also introduces an array of health benefits, including anti-inflammatory properties and antioxidants. Experiment with different combinations to discover your favorite flavors, and don't be afraid to try new spices to keep your meals interesting and delicious.

Foods to Avoid

Sugary Foods and Drinks:

As are sweetened beverages, all forms of sugar and high-sugar foods are off-limits.

Grains and Starches:

Bread, pasta, rice, and cereals are high in carbohydrates and should be avoided. This includes "healthy" grains like quinoa and oats.

Legumes: Beans:

Lentils and chickpeas are nutrient-dense but high in carbs, making them unsuitable for a ketogenic diet.

Starchy Vegetables:

Potatoes, sweet potatoes, and other root vegetables are too carbohydrate-rich for keto.

High-Carb Fruits:

Most fruits, except for certain low-carb berries, should be consumed sparingly due to their sugar content.

Processed Foods:

Many processed foods contain hidden sugars, unhealthy fats, and excessive salts.

Alcohol:

Most alcoholic beverages are high in carbs, though some spirits can be consumed in moderation.

Navigating the ketogenic diet as a woman over 60 requires a careful balance of nutrient-dense, high-fat, low-carb foods. This guide aims to provide a comprehensive overview of keto-friendly foods that support overall health, vitality, and well-being, along with a list of foods to avoid to maintain nutritional ketosis and achieve your health goals.

Accelerating Ketosis:

Practical Tips for Success

Transitioning into ketosis is a pivotal phase of the ketogenic diet, which typically takes about 48 hours. Properly adapting to a keto lifestyle can help you enter ketosis more efficiently. Below are actionable tips designed to expedite this process and enhance your ketogenic journey:

Tip 1: Limit your daily carb intake to less than 20 grams to enter ketosis swiftly.

Tip 2: Hydration is key. Aim for approximately 100 ounces \ 3 L of water per day to facilitate weight loss and metabolic processes.

Tip 3: Invest in ketosis testing strips. Monitoring your ketone levels can provide motivation and insight into how well you're adhering to the diet, especially during the initial, more challenging days.

Tip 4: Prepare for the keto flu. Symptoms like dizziness, irritability, and fatigue are common in the early days. Mitigate these by indulging in keto-friendly comfort foods like bacon, which satisfy cravings without carb intake.

Tip 5: Increase your salt intake. On a keto diet, your body sheds water more easily, leading to a rapid loss of electrolytes. Regular replenishment with sea salt can prevent feelings of lethargy or discomfort.

Tip 6: Stave off hunger proactively. Consuming high-fat, low-carb foods at the first sign of hunger helps avoid the temptation to stray from your diet plan. Simplicity is your ally; overcomplicating your meal plan can detract from the enjoyment of the diet.

Tip 7: Moderate your protein consumption. The ketogenic diet focuses on high-fat, low-carb, and moderate protein. Keeping protein intake in check is crucial to maintaining ketosis.

Tip 8: Embrace dietary fats. Eating fat to lose fat is the mantra of the keto diet. Don't shy away from healthy fats, as they are essential to your success on this diet.

Common Keto Diet Mistakes to Avoid

While mistakes are part of the learning process, awareness and preparation can help minimize their impact:

Overconsumption of Carbs:

Adhering to a daily intake of fewer than 50 grams of carbs is generally recommended for maintaining ketosis.

Excessive Protein Intake:

Remember, keto emphasizes fat over protein. Keep your protein consumption moderate.

Impatience:

Adjusting to ketosis takes time. Be patient as your body transitions from carbs to fats for energy.

Weigh Scale Obsession:

Focus on the holistic benefits of the diet rather than fixating on your weight. Keto is more than just a weight loss journey.

Insufficient Fat Intake:

The keto diet is fundamentally high-fat. Ensure you're consuming enough healthy fats daily.

Eating Processed "Keto" Foods:

Aim for a diet based on whole, natural ingredients rather than processed foods marketed as "keto-friendly."

By steering clear of these common pitfalls and adopting the tips provided, you're well on your way to a successful and enjoyable ketogenic lifestyle. Remember, the journey to ketosis is a personal one, so tailor these guidelines to fit your individual health needs and goals

Chapter III

Preparing for Your Keto Journey:

Measurements and Weight Tracking

Before embarking on your keto journey, taking initial measurements and recording your starting weight is a crucial step. This process not only sets your baseline but also helps in tracking your progress effectively, allowing you to see the tangible results of your dietary changes. Here's a guide to help you make these preliminary measurements and set the stage for a successful transformation.

Step 1: Gather Your Tools

You will need a reliable scale for measuring your weight and a soft measuring tape for taking body measurements. Ensure your scale is calibrated and placed on a hard, flat surface for accuracy. Choose a measuring tape that is flexible but not stretchable, to ensure consistency.

Step 2: Take Your Initial Weight

Time of Day: Weigh yourself at the same time of day, preferably in the morning after using the bathroom and before eating or drinking anything. This helps in getting a consistent baseline.

Clothing: Wear minimal clothing or weigh yourself without clothes for the most accurate measurement.

Record: Note down your starting weight in a journal or app where you can easily track changes over time.

Step 3: Measure Your Body

Taking body measurements can give you a more comprehensive view of your progress, as weight alone doesn't capture changes in body composition.

Key Areas to Measure: Waist, hips, chest, thighs, arms, and neck. Measuring these areas will help you understand how your body is responding to the keto diet beyond just the number on the scale.

How to Measure:

Waist:

Measure at the narrowest part of your torso, above your belly button.

Hips:

Measure at the widest part of your hips, across the hipbones.

Chest:

Measure under your arms, across the fullest part of your chest.

Thighs:

Measure around the fullest part of each thigh.

Arms:

Measure around the fullest part of each upper arm.

Neck:

Measure around the base of your neck.

Consistency: Use the same points for measurement each time to ensure consistency. It's also helpful to take measurements in front of a mirror to ensure the tape is positioned correctly.

Step 4: Document Everything

Create a dedicated record of your initial weight and measurements. Whether you prefer a digital app, a spreadsheet, or a traditional journal, choose a method that you're likely to stick with for regular updates. For your convenience, a measurement tracker is included below to facilitate the accurate recording of your measurements.

Step 5: Set Realistic Goals

Based on your starting point, set realistic, achievable goals for your keto journey. Remember, progress is more than just weight loss; it's about improving your overall health and well-being.

Step 6: Regular Check-ins

Decide on a regular interval for checking your weight and measurements. Weekly or bi-weekly check-ins can offer insight into your progress without the daily fluctuations that can occur due to various factors.

Moving Forward

With your baseline established, you're ready to start your keto journey with clarity and purpose. Remember, the numbers are just one way to gauge progress. Pay attention to how you feel, changes in energy levels, and other health improvements. Celebrate every step forward and approach your transformation with patience and positivity. Welcome to the path toward a healthier, vibrant you.

28-Day Keto Journey:

A Simple Path to Weight Loss

Nutritional Therapy Course Guidelines

Adhering to specific dietary guidelines is crucial for maximizing the benefits of a nutritional therapy course. These guidelines are designed to enhance digestion, ensure optimal nutrient intake, and support overall health. Below are the refined rules:

Chew Your Food:

Thoroughly: It's important to chew your food at least 35-40 times per bite to prevent fermentation processes in the gut.

Water Intake:

Aim to drink 1.5-2.5 liters of room temperature, pure water daily (30 ml/1 ounces per kg of ideal body weight, but not exceeding 3 liters/100 oz). Avoid drinking water during meals; instead, wait for at least 30 minutes before and after eating.

Permissible Beverages:

You may consume herbal teas, and coffee (only brewed, limited to one cup a day), without adding sugar, honey, milk, cream, or toppings as per your preference.

Meal Timings:

Breakfast between 7-9 AM (no later than 2 hours after waking up).

Second breakfast between 10 AM-12 PM.

Lunch between 1-3 PM.

Dinner between 5-8 PM (3-4 hours before bedtime).

Foods to Avoid:

Sugar, sweeteners, syrups, refined grains like semolina, white rice, couscous; salted and smoked fish, herring, caviar, dried squids, mayonnaise, sauces, sugary sodas, kvass, beer (including non-alcoholic), salted crackers, peanuts, juices, sweets, baked goods.

Fruits/Berries and Vegetables on Prescription:

Only consume certain fruits like bananas, persimmons, grapes, avocados, mangoes, watermelons, melons, and specific vegetables like potatoes, beets, carrots, pumpkins, corn, and sweet potatoes, as well as whole-grain/yeast-free bread, on a strict prescription basis.

Dairy Products:

Opt for white cheese up to 45-50% fat (Adyghe, feta, cottage cheese; mozzarella, suluguni), sour cream 15-20%, cottage cheese 3-5%, kefir up to 2.5%, sour milk up to 3.2%, and plain yogurt up to 2.5% fat - but not 0%.

Meat:

All types except for pork, lamb, duck, and goose are allowed. Visible fat and skin should be trimmed before cooking. Preferred cooking methods include steaming, stewing, baking, grilling, and boiling.

Fish:

Allowed types include pollock, cod, hake, dorado, sea bass, mackerel, flounder, pike perch, halibut, rainbow trout, sea bass, striped bass, catfish, bream, and salmon. Cooking methods: steamed, baked, grilled, boiled.

Vegetables (including frozen):

Can be consumed stewed, baked, boiled, and raw. Feel free to add balsamic or apple cider vinegar.

Grains:

Soak grains like oats (not flakes), buckwheat, unpolished rice (brown or wild), quinoa, amaranth, and millet, spelled in drinking water acidulated with lemon juice for 8-12 hours. Cook in water with a small amount (½ teaspoon per serving) of butter (82.5% fat), ghee, or coconut oil.

Pasta:

Only pasta made of hard wheat varieties is allowed.

Nuts/Seeds:

Soak almonds, hazelnuts, cashews, walnuts, flaxseeds, pumpkin seeds, and sunflower seeds in drinking water acidulated with lemon juice for 4-8 hours.

Legumes:

Soak chickpeas, peas, beans, mung beans, and lentils in drinking water acidulated with lemon juice for 8-24 hours.

Moderation in Flavorings:

Salt, spices, seasonings, onions, garlic, and superfoods can be added to taste but in moderate quantities.

Food Quantities:

All food in your diet is prescribed in grams, as prepared.

Measuring in grams eliminates the guesswork and variability that come with volume-based measurements, such as cups or tablespoons, which can vary significantly depending on the ingredient. This level of precision is particularly crucial in a weight loss journey, where every calorie and nutrient counts towards reaching your desired outcome.

Alcoholic Beverages:

Strictly as prescribed. Dry/semi-dry red and white wines are preferred.

Unlimited Consumption Allowed:

Bran (up to 30g/day), white cabbage, leafy salads, cucumbers, arugula, green onions, dill, parsley, and spinach. If feeling hungry, you may add 2-3 egg whites to your daily diet.

Skipping Meals is Prohibited:

Eat until satisfied, but avoid overeating.

Do Not Alter Your Diet Independently:

Consult with a dietitian for any dietary

Reaching the Culmination:

Your Daily Diet Menu Unveiled

As we turn the pages to the final and most pivotal section of our guide, I extend my heartfelt congratulations for embarking on this transformative journey. You've navigated through the fundamentals of nutritional wisdom, equipped yourself with the tools for effective meal planning, and are now poised at the threshold of implementing your new dietary lifestyle.

This section unveils your Daily Diet Menu, meticulously designed to blend the principles of healthy eating with the practicality of everyday life. Our approach simplifies your meal preparation routine by introducing a strategic two-day menu cycle, ensuring you enjoy a variety of nutritious meals without the daily hassle of decision-making.

By adopting this streamlined meal plan, you not only conserve valuable time but also ensure consistent adherence to a balanced and nourishing diet. It's a testament to your commitment to wellbeing, and a step forward in embracing a lifestyle that prioritizes health without sacrificing enjoyment and flavor.

So, let's raise a glass (of water, of course) to your health, success, and the exciting journey ahead. Congratulations, and here's to a happier, healthier you!

Measurement
tracker

Date:

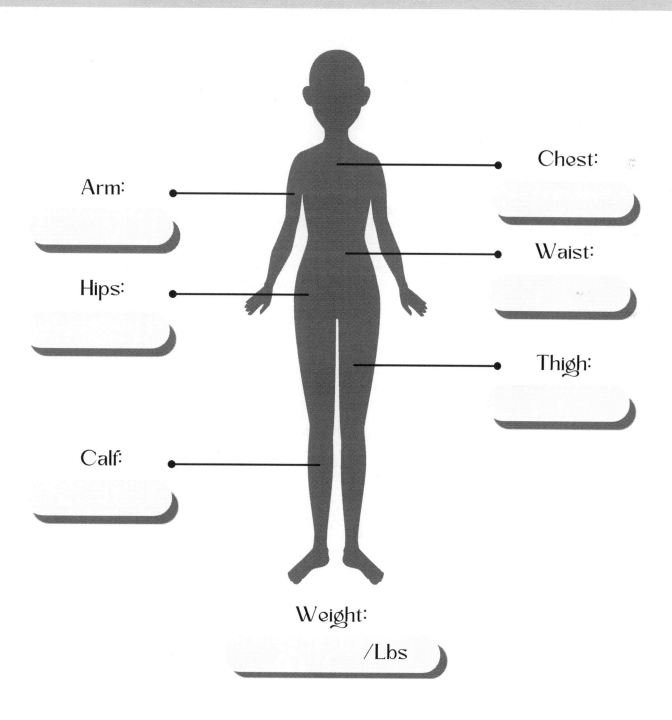

Arm:

Hips:

Calf:

Chest:

Waist:

Thigh:

Weight:

/Lbs

My notes

Date

Day

_____

_____

Day 1 & 2

Breakfast

Scrambled Eggs (2 eggs) with Tomato, Bell Pepper, and Herbs 200g

Ingredients:

- 2 eggs
- 1 medium tomato, diced
- 1/2 bell pepper, diced
- A handful of fresh herbs (such as parsley or cilantro), chopped
- Salt and pepper to taste
- 1 tablespoon olive oil

Directions:

1. Heat the olive oil in a skillet over medium heat.
2. Add the diced bell pepper and sauté for 2-3 minutes until slightly softened.
3. Add the diced tomato and sauté for another 2 minutes.
4. Beat the eggs in a bowl and pour over the vegetables in the skillet. Stir gently to combine.
5. Cook until the eggs are set but still moist, stirring occasionally.
6. Season with salt and pepper and sprinkle with fresh herbs before serving.

Day 1 & 2

Throughout the Day Addition

Nuts 20g

Opt for low-carb nuts like almonds, walnuts, or pecans.
These can be a great snack to provide energy, and healthy fats,
and keep hunger at bay without exceeding daily carbohydrate limits.

Stay hydrated, stay healthy. Drink water to fuel your body's journey

Day 1 & 2

Lunch

Chicken with Mushrooms
300g

Ingredients:

- 160g chicken breast, cut into pieces
- 150g mushrooms, sliced
- 1 tablespoon olive oil
- Salt and pepper to taste

Directions:

- Heat the olive oil in a pan over medium heat.

- Add the chicken pieces, season with salt and pepper, and cook until browned on all sides.

- Add the sliced mushrooms and continue to cook until the chicken is fully cooked and the mushrooms are tender.

Day 1 & 2

Lunch

Vegetable Salad 200g

Ingredients:

- Mixed greens (lettuce, spinach, arugula)
- Cucumber, sliced
- Cherry tomatoes, halved
- Olive oil and vinegar for dressing
- Salt and pepper to taste

Directions:

- Combine the mixed greens, cucumber, and cherry tomatoes in a bowl.

- Dress with olive oil and vinegar, then season with salt and pepper to taste.

Day 1 & 2

Dinner

Baked Fish 150g,
Vegetable Salad 220g

Ingredients:

- 150g fish fillet (such as salmon or cod)
- Olive oil
- Lemon slices
- Fresh herbs (such as dill or parsley)
- Salt and pepper to taste

For the dinner vegetable salad, follow the same preparation as the lunch salad, adjusting the quantity to 220g.

Directions:

- Preheat the oven to 200°C (392°F).
- Place the fish fillet on a baking sheet lined with parchment paper.
- Drizzle with olive oil and season with salt and pepper.
- Top with lemon slices and fresh herbs.
- Bake in the preheated oven for 12-15 minutes, or until the fish is cooked through and flakes easily with a fork.

Day 3 & 4

Breakfast

Cheese Pancakes/Bake 180g

Ingredients:

- 1 cup cottage cheese (drained)
- 2 eggs
- 2 tablespoons all-purpose flour (for a keto option, use almond or coconut flour)
- 1 tablespoon erythritol or another sweetener (optional)
- Vanilla extract to taste
- A pinch of salt
- Butter or oil for frying

Directions:

- In a mixing bowl, combine the cottage cheese, eggs, flour, sweetener (if using), vanilla extract, and a pinch of salt. Mix until well combined.

- Heat a non-stick skillet over medium heat and add a little butter or oil.

- Scoop the batter onto the skillet to form small pancakes. Fry until golden brown on both sides.
- Alternatively, for a bake, pour the mixture into a greased baking dish and bake at 180°C (356°F) for about 20 minutes or until set and lightly golden.

Day 3 & 4

Throughout the Day Addition

Cheese: 50g
of your favorite hard or soft cheese,
ensuring it's low in carbs and fits
within your daily macros.

.

Stay hydrated, stay healthy. Drink water to fuel your body's journey

Day 3 & 4

Lunch

Spaghetti with Cheese 200g

Ingredients:

- 200g spaghetti (use keto-friendly or whole-grain spaghetti for a healthier option)
- 1/2 cup grated cheese (Parmesan or your choice)
- Salt and pepper to taste
- Olive oil

Directions:

- Cook the spaghetti according to package instructions until al dente. Drain.

- Toss the hot spaghetti with a bit of olive oil and grated cheese. Season with salt and pepper to taste.

Day 3 & 4

Lunch

Ajapsandali
(Georgian Vegetable Stew) 200g

Ingredients:

- 1 eggplant, cubed
- 1 bell pepper, chopped
- 1 tomato, chopped
- 1 onion, chopped
- 1 garlic clove, minced
- Fresh herbs (coriander, parsley)
- Salt, pepper, and spices to taste
- Olive oil

Directions:

- In a large pan, heat olive oil over medium heat. Sauté the onion and garlic until softened.
- Add eggplant and bell pepper, and cook until they start to soften.
- Add the tomato, season with salt, pepper, and spices, and simmer until vegetables are tender. Stir in fresh herbs before serving

Day 3 & 4

Dinner

Potatoes with Mushrooms and Herbs 270g

Ingredients:

- 1medium potatoes, cubed
- 200g mushrooms, sliced
- Fresh herbs (parsley, dill)
- Salt and pepper to taste
- Olive oil

Directions:

- Boil the potatoes until tender, then drain.
- In a pan, sauté the mushrooms in olive oil until golden. Add the boiled potatoes, season with salt, pepper, and herbs, and cook until crispy.

Day 3 & 4

Dinner

Boiled Beets with Feta (Garlic Optional) 150g

Ingredients:

- 2 medium beets, boiled and cubed
- 1/2 cup feta cheese, crumbled
- 1 garlic clove, minced (optional)
- Olive oil

Directions:

- Combine the cubed beets and crumbled feta in a bowl. Add minced garlic if using.
- Drizzle with olive oil before serving.

Day 5 & 6

Breakfast

Zucchini Fritters 200g

Ingredients:

- 2 medium zucchinis, grated
- 1 large egg
- 1/2 cup almond flour
- 1/4 cup grated Parmesan cheese
- Salt and pepper to taste
- Olive oil for frying

Directions:

- Squeeze the grated zucchini with a clean towel to remove excess moisture.

- In a bowl, mix the zucchini, egg, almond flour, Parmesan cheese, salt, and pepper.

- Heat olive oil in a skillet over medium heat. Scoop tablespoons of the zucchini mixture into the skillet, flattening them into fritters.

- Fry until golden brown on both sides, about 2-3 minutes per side. Serve hot.

Day 5 & 6

Throughout the Day Addition
Berries 300g

To stay within keto guidelines, opt for low-carb berries like strawberries, raspberries, or blueberries.
These can be enjoyed as a midday snack, providing sweetness and nutrients without significantly increasing your carb intake

Stay hydrated, stay healthy.
Drink water to fuel your body's journey

Day 5 & 6

Lunch

Meat Patties/Chicken 130g

Ingredients:

- 130g ground beef or chicken breast
- Salt, pepper, and spices to taste
- Olive oil for cooking

Directions:

- Season the ground beef or chicken breast with salt, pepper, and spices.

- Form the beef into patties or slice the chicken breast. Cook in a skillet with olive oil until fully cooked and golden brown.

Day 5 & 6

Lunch

Keto Greek Salad 200g

Ingredients:

- 1 cup diced cucumber
- 1/2 cup cherry tomatoes, halved
- 1/4 cup sliced red onion
- 1/4 cup olives
- 1/2 cup crumbled feta cheese
- 2 tablespoons olive oil
- 1 tablespoon apple cider vinegar
- Salt and pepper to taste

Directions:

- Season the ground beef or chicken breast with salt, pepper, and spices.

- Form the beef into patties or slice the chicken breast. Cook in a skillet with olive oil until fully cooked and golden brown.

Day 5 & 6

Dinner

Leafy Salad with Tuna, Egg, and Feta 300g

Ingredients:

- 2 cups mixed leafy greens
- 1 can of tuna in olive oil, drained
- 2 hard-boiled eggs, sliced
- 1/2 cup crumbled feta cheese
- Olive oil and lemon juice for dressing
- Salt and pepper to taste

Directions:

- Arrange the mixed leafy greens on a plate.

- Top with tuna, sliced hard-boiled eggs, and crumbled feta cheese.

- Drizzle with olive oil and a squeeze of lemon juice. Season with salt and pepper to taste. Toss gently to combine.

Day 7 & 8

Breakfast

Keto-Friendly Seed Bread, Half an Avocado, Fried Eggs (2 eggs), Vegetables

Ingredients:

- 1 slice of keto-friendly seed or almond flour bread
- 1/2 ripe avocado
- 2 eggs
- Mixed vegetables (such as spinach, bell peppers, and mushrooms)
- Olive oil for cooking
- Salt and pepper to taste

Directions:

- Toast the keto-friendly bread slice until golden.
- In a skillet, heat a bit of olive oil and sauté the mixed vegetables until tender. Remove and set aside.
- In the same skillet, fry the two eggs to your preference. Season with salt and pepper.
- Serve the fried eggs on top of the toasted keto bread, accompanied by the sautéed vegetables and sliced avocado on the side.

Day 7 & 8

Throughout the Day Addition

Cheese: 50g
of your favorite hard or soft cheese,
ensuring it's low in carbs and fits
within your daily macros.

Stay hydrated, stay healthy.
Drink water to fuel your body's journey

Day 7 & 8

Lunch

Leafy Salad with Turkey, Cheese, and Nuts 300 g

Ingredients:

- 2 cups mixed leafy greens (such as spinach and arugula)
- 130g cooked turkey breast, sliced
- A small handful of keto-friendly cheese, cubed (such as feta or goat cheese)
- A small handful of nuts (such as walnuts or almonds), roughly chopped
- Olive oil and vinegar for dressing
- Salt and pepper to taste

Directions:

- Toss the mixed leafy greens, sliced turkey, cheese, and nuts in a large salad bowl.

- Drizzle with olive oil and vinegar, then season with salt and pepper to taste.

- Toss gently to combine all ingredients and serve.

Day 7 & 8

Dinner

Braised Rabbit 150g

Ingredients:

- 150g rabbit meat, cut into pieces
- Olive oil for browning
- Herbs and spices (such as rosemary, thyme, garlic)
- Salt and pepper to taste
- Chicken or vegetable broth for braising

Directions:

- Season the rabbit pieces with salt, pepper, and herbs. Brown them in olive oil in a heavy skillet.

- Add enough broth to partially cover the meat. Cover and simmer gently until the rabbit is tender, about 1-1.5 hours.

- Adjust seasoning as needed and serve.

Day 7 & 8

Dinner

Fresh Vegetable Salad with Cabbage 200g

Ingredients:

- 1 cup shredded cabbage
- 1/2 cup mixed vegetables (such as cucumber, radishes, and bell peppers), chopped
- Olive oil and lemon juice for dressing
- Salt and pepper to taste

Directions:

- Combine the shredded cabbage and chopped vegetables in a salad bowl.

- Dress with olive oil and lemon juice, then season with salt and pepper to taste.

- Toss well and serve alongside the braised rabbit.

Day 9 & 10

Breakfast

Keto Porridge, Cod Liver, and Vegetables 200g

Ingredients:

- 1/4 cup chia seeds
- 1/2 cup almond milk (or coconut milk)
- 1 tablespoon flaxseed meal
- Sweetener to taste (optional)

- 50g cod liver (canned is fine)
- 150g mixed vegetables (e.g., spinach, mushrooms, bell peppers)
- Olive oil, salt, and pepper for cooking

Directions:

- Mix chia seeds, almond milk, and flaxseed meal in a bowl. Let sit for 10 minutes until the mixture reaches a porridge-like consistency. Sweeten if desired.

- Sauté the mixed vegetables in olive oil until tender. Season with salt and pepper.

- Serve the keto porridge topped with cod liver and accompanied by the sautéed vegetables.

Day 9 & 10

Throughout the Day Addition

Nuts 20g

Opt for low-carb nuts like almonds, walnuts, or pecans.
These can be a great snack to provide energy, and healthy fats,
and keep hunger at bay without exceeding daily carbohydrate limits.

Stay hydrated, stay healthy. Drink water to fuel your body's journey

Day 9 & 10

Lunch

Ajapsandali (Georgian Vegetable Stew), Keto-Friendly Side 300g

Ingredients:

- 1 eggplant, cubed
- 1 bell pepper, chopped
- 1 tomato, chopped
- 1 onion, chopped
- 1 garlic clove, minced
- Fresh herbs (coriander, parsley)
- Salt, pepper, and spices to taste
- Olive oil

Directions:

- In a large pan, heat olive oil over medium heat. Sauté the onion and garlic until softened.

- Add eggplant and bell pepper, and cook until they start to soften.

- Add the tomato, season with salt, pepper, and spices, and simmer until vegetables are tender.

- Stir in fresh herbs before serving

Day 9 & 10

Dinner

Stewed Vegetables with Seafood
350g

Ingredients:

- 150g mixed seafood (shrimp, scallops, squid)
- 200g mixed low-carb vegetables (zucchini, asparagus, bell peppers)
- Olive oil, garlic, herbs (e.g., parsley, dill)
- Salt and pepper to taste

Directions:

- Heat olive oil in a large pan. Add garlic and sauté until fragrant.

- Add the mixed vegetables and cook until slightly tender.

- Add the seafood and cook until just done. Season with herbs, salt, and pepper.

- Serve the stewed vegetables with seafood, ensuring a flavorful and satisfying dinner.

Measurement tracker

Date:

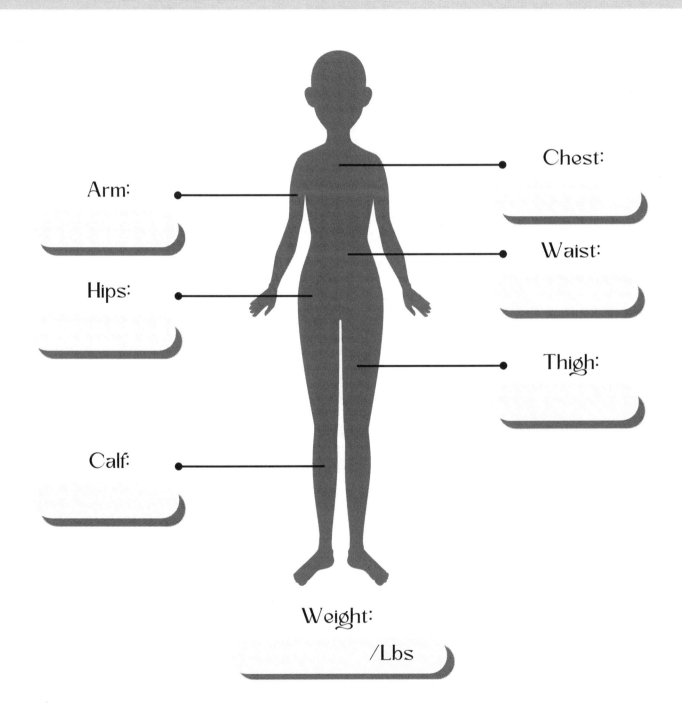

Arm:

Hips:

Calf:

Chest:

Waist:

Thigh:

Weight:

/Lbs

My notes

Date

Day

_____

_____

Day 11 & 12

Breakfast

Cauliflower in Egg 300g, Avocado 30g

Ingredients:

- 260g cauliflower florets
- 2 large eggs, beaten
- 30g avocado, sliced

Directions:

- Dip the cauliflower florets into the beaten eggs, ensuring they are well coated.

- Fry the egg-coated cauliflower in a preheated skillet with a bit of olive oil until golden brown on all sides.

- Serve the cauliflower with slices of avocado on the side.

Day 11 & 12

Throughout the Day Addition

Berries 300g

To stay within keto guidelines, opt for low-carb berries like strawberries, raspberries, or blueberries.
These can be enjoyed as a midday snack, providing sweetness and nutrients without significantly increasing your carb intake

Stay hydrated, stay healthy. Drink water to fuel your body's journey

Day 11 & 12

Lunch

Pork Cutlet 120g, Caprese Salad 350g

Ingredients:

- 120g pork loin, tenderized into a cutlet
- Salt, pepper, and herbs for seasoning

Ingredients:

- 200g ripe tomatoes, sliced
- 150g fresh mozzarella cheese, sliced
- Fresh basil leaves
- Olive oil and balsamic vinegar (optional) for dressing
- ·Salt and pepper to taste

Directions:

- Season the pork cutlet with salt, pepper, and your choice of herbs. Grill or pan-fry until fully cooked and golden brown.

- Assemble the Caprese salad by alternating slices of tomato and mozzarella cheese on a plate, adding basil leaves between layers. Drizzle with olive oil and a small amount of balsamic vinegar if desired. Season with salt and pepper.

Day 11 & 12

Dinner

Fish/Seafood 130g, Grilled Vegetables with Pesto Sauce 180g

Ingredients:

- 130g of your choice of fish or mixed seafood
- Olive oil, lemon juice, salt, and pepper for seasoning

Ingredients:

- Mixed vegetables (e.g., zucchini, bell peppers, asparagus) totaling 180g
- Homemade or store-bought keto-friendly pesto sauce

Directions:

- Season the fish or seafood with olive oil, lemon juice, salt, and pepper. Grill or bake until cooked through.
- Grill the mixed vegetables until tender and slightly charred. Toss the grilled vegetables in pesto sauce until well coated.
- Serve the fish or seafood alongside the pesto-coated grilled vegetables for a flavorful and nutritious dinner.

Day 13 & 14

Breakfast

Keto Cheesecake/Bake 120g

Ingredients:

- 1 cup almond flour (for the base)
- 1/4 cup butter, melted
- 2 tbsp erythritol (for the base)
- 16 oz cream cheese, softened
- 1/2 cup erythritol (for the filling)
- 2 eggs
- 1 tsp vanilla extract

For the cappuccino, use unsweetened almond milk or heavy cream instead of regular milk to keep it keto-friendly.

Directions:

- Preheat the oven to 350°F (175°C). Mix almond flour, melted butter, and 2 tbsp erythritol, and press into the bottom of a greased baking dish to form the base.
- Beat the cream cheese, 1/2 cup erythritol, eggs, and vanilla extract until smooth. Pour over the base.
- Bake for 45-50 minutes or until set. Allow to cool before serving. Serve a 120g portion for breakfast.

Day 13 & 14

Throughout the Day Addition

Cheese: 50g

of your favorite hard or soft cheese,
ensuring it's low in carbs and fits within your daily macros.

Stay hydrated, stay healthy. Drink water to fuel your body's journey

Day 13 & 14

Lunch

Lasagna with Cabbage Leaves 180g, Vegetables 160g

Ingredients:

- Cabbage leaves (blanched) as lasagna sheets
- Ground beef or pork
- Homemade tomato sauce (use fresh tomatoes, garlic, and herbs, cooked down)
- Ricotta and mozzarella cheese
- Salt, pepper, and Italian seasoning

Directions:

- Layer blanched cabbage leaves, cooked ground meat seasoned with salt, pepper, and Italian seasoning, spoonfuls of tomato sauce, and dollops of ricotta in a baking dish. Sprinkle mozzarella between layers.
- Bake at 375°F (190°C) for 25-30 minutes until bubbly and golden.
- Serve with a side of sautéed low-carb vegetables like zucchini or broccoli (160g).

Day 13 & 14

Dinner

Leafy Salad with Smoked Salmon, Avocado, and Cashews 270g

Ingredients:

- Mixed leafy greens (spinach, arugula, lettuce)
- 100g smoked salmon
- 1 small avocado, sliced
- A handful of cashews
- Olive oil and lemon juice for dressing
- •Salt and pepper to taste

Directions:

- Toss mixed leafy greens, smoked salmon, avocado slices, and cashews in a large salad bowl.

- Dress with olive oil and lemon juice, then season with salt and pepper to taste.

Day 15 & 16

Breacfast

Keto Grain Bread, Pork Belly 20g
(or Avocado 40g),
Sunny-side up/Fried Egg 1 pc, Vegetables

Ingredients:

- 1 cup almond flour
- 1/2 cup flaxseed meal
- 1/4 cup psyllium husk powder
- 1 tsp baking powder
- Salt to taste
- 4 eggs
- 1/2 cup warm water

Directions:

- Mix almond flour, flaxseed meal, psyllium husk, baking powder, and salt.
- Add eggs and warm water, mixing to form a dough.
- Shape into a loaf and bake at 350°F (175°C) for 45-50 minutes.
- Serve a 30g slice of this bread with either 20g pork belly or 40g avocado, alongside a fried egg and a selection of low-carb vegetables such as spinach or bell peppers.

Day 15 & 16

Throughout the Day Addition

Berries 300g

To stay within keto guidelines, opt for low-carb berries like strawberries, raspberries, or blueberries.
These can be enjoyed as a midday snack, providing sweetness and nutrients without significantly increasing your carb intake

Stay hydrated, stay healthy. Drink water to fuel your body's journey

Day 15 & 16

Lunch

Keto porridge 200g

Ingredients:

- 2 tablespoons coconut flour
- 2 tablespoons almond flour
- 1 tablespoon flaxseed meal
- 1 tablespoon chia seeds
- 1/2 cup unsweetened almond milk (or coconut milk for a creamier texture)
- 1/2 cup water
- 1/4 teaspoon cinnamon (optional for flavor)
- Sweetener to taste (e.g., erythritol, stevia, or monk fruit sweetener)
- A pinch of salt

•Optional Toppings:
•A handful of berries (raspberries, strawberries, or blueberries)
•Sliced almonds or walnuts
•Unsweetened shredded coconut
•A dollop of unsweetened almond butter or peanut butter
•A sprinkle of cinnamon or cocoa powder

Directions:

- Combine Dry Ingredients: In a small saucepan, mix the coconut flour, almond flour, flaxseed meal, chia seeds, cinnamon (if using), and a pinch of salt.
- Add Liquids: Pour in the almond milk and water. Stir well to combine and ensure there are no lumps.
- Cook: Place the saucepan over medium heat. Cook the mixture, stirring frequently, for about 5-7 minutes or until the porridge thickens to your desired consistency. The chia seeds and flaxseed meal will help thicken the porridge as they absorb the liquid.
- Sweeten: Once the porridge has thickened, remove it from the heat and stir in your preferred sweetener to taste.
- Serve: Pour the keto porridge into a bowl. Top with your choice of optional toppings for added texture, flavor, and nutritional value.

Day 15 & 16

Dinner

Fish Cakes 100g, Roasted Vegetables 200g

Ingredients:

- 100g groundfish (any low-fat variety)
- 1 egg (as a binder)
- Almond flour (for binding and coating)
- Seasonings (salt, pepper, herbs)
- Olive oil for frying

Ingredients:

- 200g mixed low-carb vegetables (zucchini, bell peppers, asparagus)
- Olive oil
- Salt and herbs for seasoning

Directions:

- Mix groundfish, egg, a small amount of almond flour, and seasonings. Form into patties and lightly coat with almond flour.
- Fry in olive oil until golden and cooked through.
- Toss vegetables in olive oil and seasonings. Roast at 400°F (200°C) until tender and slightly caramelized.

Day 17 & 18

Breakfast

Cauliflower rice 120g, Green Beans with Bell Pepper 150g

Ingredients:

- Cauliflower rice,
- Olive oil
- Salt and pepper to taste

Ingredients:

- 150g green beans, trimmed
- 1 bell pepper, sliced
- Olive oil
- •Salt and pepper to taste

Directions:

- For the cauliflower rice, heat olive oil in a pan over medium heat. Add the grated cauliflower, season with salt and pepper, and sauté until tender and slightly crispy.

- For the green beans and bell pepper, heat olive oil in another pan, add green beans and bell pepper, season with salt and pepper, and cook until vegetables are tender but still crisp.

Day 17 & 18

Throughout the Day Addition:

Nuts 20g

Opt for low-carb nuts like almonds, walnuts, or pecans. These can be a great snack to provide energy, and healthy fats, and keep hunger at bay without exceeding daily carbohydrate limits.

Stay hydrated, stay healthy.
Drink water to fuel your body's journey

Day 17 & 18

Lunch

Avocado Chicken Salad 130g, Vegetable Salad with Guacamole 200g

Ingredients:

- 130g cooked chicken breast, shredded
- 1 ripe avocado, mashed
- A squeeze of lemon juice
- Salt and pepper to taste

Ingredients:

- Mixed greens (lettuce, spinach, arugula)
- Cucumber, cherry tomatoes, sliced
- Prepared guacamole or mashed avocado with lime juice, salt, and pepper

Directions:

- For the avocado chicken salad, mix shredded chicken with mashed avocado, and add lemon juice, salt, and pepper. Adjust seasoning to taste.

- Assemble the vegetable salad with mixed greens and sliced veggies. Top with a dollop of guacamole or mashed avocado.

Day 17 & 18

Dinner

Creamy Garlic Shrimp 120g, Fresh Vegetables 180g

Ingredients:

- 120g shrimp, peeled and deveined
- 2 cloves garlic, minced
- 1/4 cup heavy cream
- 2 tablespoons butter
- Salt and pepper to taste
- Fresh parsley, chopped

Ingredients:

- 180g mixed fresh vegetables (cucumber, radishes, bell peppers)
- Olive oil and vinegar for dressing
- Salt and pepper to taste

Directions:

- In a pan, melt butter over medium heat, add garlic, and sauté until fragrant.
- Add shrimp, season with salt and pepper, and cook until pink.

- Pour in heavy cream, stir to combine, and simmer until sauce thickens.
- Garnish with parsley.

- Serve the creamy garlic shrimp with a side of fresh vegetables dressed lightly with olive oil and vinegar.

Day 19 & 20

Breakfast

Scrambled Eggs with Zucchini 300g

Ingredients:

- 2 eggs
- 200g zucchini, sliced or grated
- Salt and pepper to taste
- Olive oil or butter for cooking

Directions:

- Heat a bit of olive oil or butter in a skillet over medium heat.
- Add the zucchini and sauté until slightly tender.
- Beat the eggs and pour over the zucchini in the skillet. Stir gently to combine.
- Cook until the eggs are fully set. Season with salt and pepper to taste.

Day 19 & 20

Snacks Throughout the Day:

Cheese:

50g of your favorite hard or soft cheese,

ensuring it's low in carbs and fits within your daily macros.

Stay hydrated, stay healthy.
Drink water to fuel your body's journey

Day 19 & 20

Lunch

Poultry Meat 130g
Vegetable Salad with Herbs 220g

Ingredients:

- 130g chicken or turkey breast
- Olive oil
- Salt, pepper, and your choice of herbs

Ingredients:

- Mixed leafy greens
- Cucumber, tomatoes, bell pepper (any low-carb vegetables)
- Fresh herbs like parsley, dill, or basil
- Olive oil and lemon juice or vinegar for dressing
- Salt and pepper to taste

Directions:

- Season the poultry meat with salt, pepper, and herbs. Grill or bake until fully cooked and juicy.
- Toss the mixed leafy greens and chopped vegetables with fresh herbs. Dress with olive oil and lemon juice or vinegar. Season with salt and pepper.

Day 19 & 20

Dinner

Fish 110g,
Grilled Vegetables with Pesto Sauce 200g

Ingredients:

- 110g of your choice of fish (salmon, cod, tilapia)
- Olive oil
- Salt, pepper, and lemon slices

Ingredients:

- 200g mixed vegetables (zucchini, bell peppers, asparagus, eggplant)
- Homemade or store-bought keto-friendly pesto sauce
- Olive oil
- Salt and pepper

Directions:

- Season the fish with olive oil, salt, and pepper. Place lemon slices on top. Bake or grill until the fish flakes easily with a fork.

- Slice the vegetables, toss with olive oil, salt, and pepper, and grill until tender and charred.

- Toss the grilled vegetables in pesto sauce until well coated.

Measurement tracker

S M T W T F S

Date:

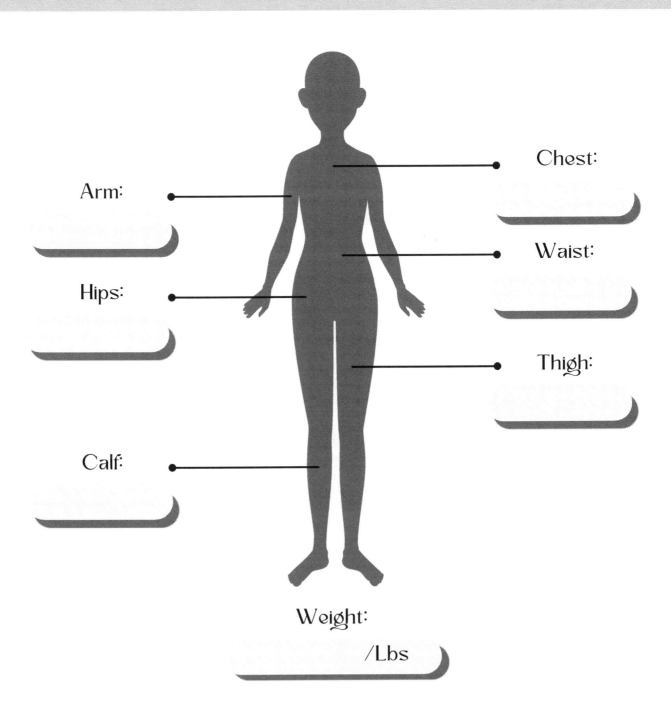

Arm:

Chest:

Waist:

Hips:

Thigh:

Calf:

Weight:

/Lbs

My notes

Date

Day

_____

_____

Day 21 & 22

Breakfast

Keto Cheese Pancakes with Berry Sauce 200g

Ingredients:

- 1 cup almond flour
- 2 eggs
- 1 cup ricotta cheese or any low-carb, high-fat cheese
- Erythritol or another keto-friendly sweetener to taste
- Butter or coconut oil for frying

Ingredients:

- 1/2 cup mixed berries (raspberries, strawberries, blackberries), fresh or frozen
- Erythritol to taste
- A splash of water

Directions:

- Mix almond flour, eggs, ricotta cheese, and sweetener in a bowl until well combined.
- Heat butter or coconut oil in a skillet over medium heat. Drop spoonfuls of the batter into the skillet, cooking until golden brown on both sides.
- For the sauce, combine berries, sweetener, and water in a small saucepan. Simmer until the berries break down into a sauce. Pour over pancakes.

Day 21 & 22

Midday Addition

Berries 350g

Opt for low-carb options like berries
(strawberries, raspberries, blackberries)
or a small serving of other keto-friendly fruits
(avocado, olives) to stay within ketogenic guidelines,
enjoying them as a snack in the first half of the day.

Stay hydrated, stay healthy.
Drink water to fuel your body's journey

Day 21 & 22

Lunch

Keto Radishes and Cabbage Salad 360g

Ingredients: Ingredients:

- 160 g radishes, quartered
- Olive oil
- Salt and pepper
- Fresh dill

- 200g shredded cabbage
- 1 cucumber, sliced
- Fresh herbs (dill, parsley)
- Olive oil and apple cider vinegar for dressing
- Salt and pepper to taste

Directions:

- Toss radishes with olive oil, salt, and pepper. Roast at 400°F (200°C) until tender and slightly crispy, about 20-25 minutes. Sprinkle with fresh dill before serving.
- Combine shredded cabbage, sliced cucumber, and fresh herbs. Dress with olive oil and apple cider vinegar, then season with salt and pepper.

Day 21 & 22

Dinner

Mushroom Sauté 140g
and Fresh Vegetable Sauté 200g

Ingredients:

- 140g mushrooms, sliced
- Olive oil
- Garlic, minced
- Fresh herbs (thyme, parsley)

Ingredients:

- 200g mixed low-carb vegetables (zucchini, bell peppers, spinach)
- Olive oil
- Salt and pepper

Directions:

- Sauté mushrooms in olive oil with garlic and herbs until tender and golden. Season with salt and pepper.
- In another pan, sauté mixed vegetables in olive oil until tender. Season with salt and pepper.

Day 23 & 24

Breakfast

Zucchini Fritters 220g

Ingredients:

- 2 medium zucchinis, grated
- 2 eggs
- 1/2 cup almond flour
- 1/4 cup grated Parmesan cheese
- Salt and pepper to taste
- Olive oil for frying

Directions:

- Squeeze excess moisture from the grated zucchini using a clean towel.

- In a bowl, mix the zucchini with eggs, almond flour, Parmesan, salt, and pepper until combined.

- Heat olive oil in a skillet over medium heat. Scoop the mixture to form fritters and fry until golden brown on both sides. Set aside on a paper towel to drain any excess oil.

Day 23 & 24

Throughout the Day Addition:

Nuts 20g

Opt for low-carb nuts like almonds, walnuts, or pecans. These can be a great snack to provide energy, and healthy fats, and keep hunger at bay without exceeding daily carbohydrate limits.

Stay hydrated, stay healthy.
Drink water to fuel your body's journey

Day 23 & 24

Lunch

Leafy Salad with Meat 120g and Tomatoes 330g

Ingredients:

- 120g cooked beef, chicken, or turkey, sliced
- Mixed leafy greens (e.g., spinach, arugula, romaine)
- 1 large tomato, sliced
- Olive oil and vinegar or lemon juice for dressing
- Salt and pepper to taste

Directions:

- On a large plate, arrange a bed of mixed leafy greens.
- Top with sliced meat and tomatoes.
- Drizzle with olive oil and vinegar or lemon juice, then season with salt and pepper to taste.

Day 23 & 24

Dinner

Seafood in Creamy Garlic Sauce 100g, Vegetable Salad 200g

Ingredients:

- 100g mixed seafood (shrimp, scallops, squid)
- 2 cloves garlic, minced
- 1/4 cup heavy cream
- 2 tablespoons butter
- Salt and pepper to taste
- Fresh herbs for garnish

Ingredients:

- 200g mixed vegetables (e.g., cucumber, bell peppers, avocado)
- Olive oil and lemon juice for dressing
- Salt and pepper to taste

Directions:

- In a skillet, melt butter over medium heat and sauté garlic until fragrant. Add seafood and cook until pink and opaque.

- Lower the heat and stir in heavy cream. Simmer until the sauce thickens. Season with salt and pepper.

- Toss mixed vegetables with olive oil and lemon juice, seasoning with salt and pepper for the salad.

Day 25 & 26

Breakfast

Keto Avocado and Egg Toast

Ingredients:

- 1 large avocado
- 2 eggs, fried or poached
- 2 slices of keto-friendly bread (made from almond flour or coconut flour)
- Salt, pepper, and chili flakes to taste
- Optional: A sprinkle of feta cheese or a few slices of bacon for extra flavor

Directions:

- Toast the keto-friendly bread slices until golden brown.
- Mash the avocado and spread it evenly on each slice of toast.
- Top each slice with a fried or poached egg.
- Season with salt, pepper, and chili flakes. Add feta cheese or bacon if desired.

Day 25 & 26
Midday Addition

Snacks Throughout the Day:

Cheese:

50g of your favorite hard or soft cheese,

ensuring it's low in carbs and fits within your daily macros.

Day 25 & 26

Lunch

Grilled Chicken Salad with Mixed Greens 200g

Ingredients:

- 120g chicken breast, grilled and sliced
- 2 cups mixed greens (arugula, spinach, romaine lettuce)
- 1/4 cup cherry tomatoes, halved
- 1/4 avocado, sliced
- 2 tablespoons olive oil
- 1 tablespoon apple cider vinegar
- Salt and pepper to taste
- Optional toppings: Sliced almonds, cheese crumbles

Directions:

- In a large salad bowl, toss the mixed greens, cherry tomatoes, and avocado slices.

- In a small bowl, whisk together olive oil, apple cider vinegar, salt, and pepper to create the dressing.

- Add the grilled chicken slices to the salad. Pour the dressing over the salad and toss to combine.

- Garnish with optional toppings like sliced almonds or cheese crumbles.

Day 25 & 26

Dinner

Creamy Garlic Shrimp with Zucchini Noodles 200g

Ingredients:

- 100g shrimp, peeled and deveined
- 2 zucchinis, spiralized into noodles
- 2 tablespoons butter
- 2 cloves garlic, minced
- 1/4 cup heavy cream
- Salt and pepper to taste
- Fresh parsley, chopped for garnish

Directions:

- In a pan, melt butter over medium heat. Add garlic and sauté until fragrant.

- Add the shrimp and cook until they turn pink and are cooked through.

- Stir in the heavy cream, and let it simmer for a few minutes until the sauce thickens. Season with salt and pepper.

- In another pan, sauté the spiralized zucchini noodles in a bit of olive oil for 1-2 minutes until just tender.

-

- Serve the creamy garlic shrimp over the zucchini noodles. Garnish with chopped parsley.

Day 27 & 28

Breakfast

Keto-friendly omelet 200g

Ingredients:

- 3 large eggs (approx. 150g)
- 2 tablespoons of heavy cream (for fluffiness, optional)
- Salt and pepper, to taste
- 1 tablespoon of unsalted butter or olive oil, for cooking

Filling Options:
- 1/4 cup shredded cheese (cheddar, mozzarella, or your choice)
- 1/4 cup chopped spinach
- 2 tablespoons chopped bell peppers
- 2 tablespoons diced cooked bacon or ham

For the Sides:
- 1/2 avocado, sliced (approx. 100g)
- A handful of cherry tomatoes (keep to a minimum for strict keto)

Directions:

- Prepare the Filling:
  - Cook bacon or ham until crispy; set aside. Sauté spinach and bell peppers in the same pan until tender; combine with bacon/ham.
- Make the Omelet:
  - Whisk eggs, heavy cream (optional), salt, and pepper. Cook in a buttered or oiled skillet over medium heat until edges set. Add cheese and filling to one half, then fold and cook until cheese melts.
- Prepare the Sides:
  - Slice the avocado and, if using, prepare cherry tomatoes.
- Serve:
  - Plate the omelet with avocado slices and cherry tomatoes on the side.

Day 27 & 28
Midday Addition

Mixed Nuts and Berries 300g

Ingredients:

•A handful of mixed nuts (almonds, walnuts, pecans)
•A small bowl of mixed berries (strawberries, raspberries, blackberries)

Preparation:
•Mix the nuts and berries in a bowl or portable container for an easy, nutritious snack.

.

Day 27 & 28

Lunch

Zucchini Noodles with Pesto and Grilled Chicken 300g

Ingredients:

- 2 medium zucchinis, spiralized into noodles
- 1 tablespoon of olive oil

For the Pesto:
- 2 cups of fresh basil leaves
- 1/2 cup of grated Parmesan cheese
- 1/3 cup of olive oil
- 1/4 cup of pine nuts (or walnuts)
- 2 garlic cloves
- Salt and pepper to taste

For the Chicken:
- 2 boneless, skinless chicken breasts (about 150g)
- Salt and pepper
- 1 tablespoon of olive oil, for grilling

Day 27 & 28

Lunch

Zucchini Noodles with Pesto and Grilled Chicken 300g

Directions:

Prepare the Chicken:
- Season the chicken breasts with salt and pepper.
- Heat a grill pan over medium-high heat and brush it with olive oil. Grill the chicken for about 5-7 minutes on each side or until fully cooked and the internal temperature reaches 165°F (74°C). Remove from the grill and let it rest before slicing it thinly.

Make the Pesto:
- In a food processor, combine the basil leaves, Parmesan cheese, pine nuts, garlic cloves, and a pinch of salt and pepper. Pulse until coarsely chopped.
- Gradually add the olive oil while the processor is running until the pesto is smooth. Adjust salt and pepper to taste.

Cook the Zucchini Noodles:
- Heat a large skillet over medium heat and add 1 tablespoon of olive oil. Add the spiralized zucchini noodles and sauté for about 2-3 minutes until just tender. Be careful not to overcook them to prevent them from becoming soggy.
- Combine and Serve:
- Toss the zucchini noodles with the pesto until evenly coated. Serve the noodles with sliced grilled chicken on top.

Day 27 & 28

Dinner

Lemon Herb Salmon with Asparagus 350g

Ingredients:

- 150g salmon fillet
- 100g fresh asparagus, ends trimmed
- 1 tablespoon olive oil
- Salt and pepper to taste
- 1/2 lemon, for both juice and zest
- 1 garlic clove, minced
- 1 teaspoon fresh dill, chopped (or 1/2 teaspoon dried dill)
- 1 teaspoon fresh parsley, chopped (optional for garnish)

Directions:

- Preheat your oven to 400°F (200°C).
- Place the salmon fillet and trimmed asparagus on the prepared baking sheet. Drizzle olive oil over both, and season generously with salt and pepper. Add the minced garlic atop the salmon.
- Squeeze lemon juice over the salmon and asparagus.
- Bake in the preheated oven for about 12-15 minutes, or until the salmon flakes easily with a fork and the asparagus is tender but still crisp.
- Garnish the salmon with fresh parsley if desired before serving.

Measurement Tracker

S M T W T F S

Date:

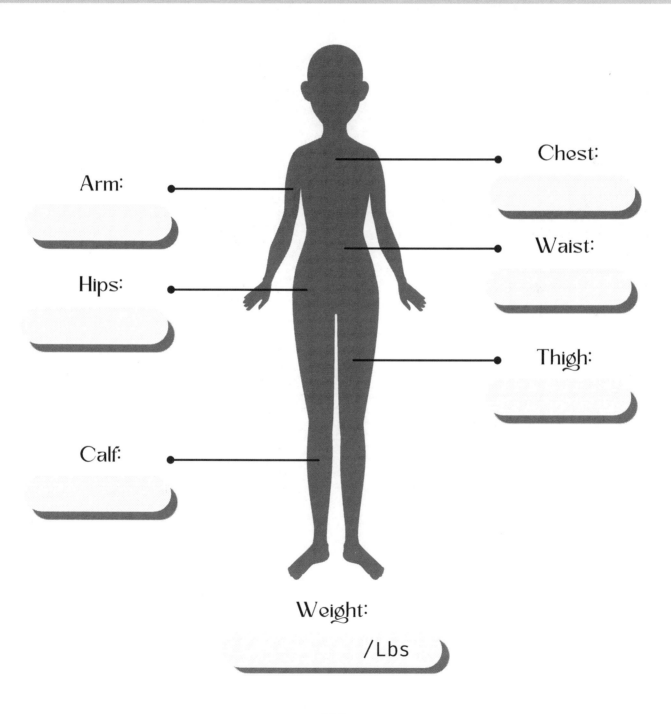

Arm:

Hips:

Calf:

Chest:

Waist:

Thigh:

Weight:

/Lbs

My notes

Date

Day

_____

_____

Conclusion

As we draw this guide to a close, let's pause to reflect on the journey we've embarked upon together. The ketogenic diet stands as a beacon of hope, particularly for women over 60, offering a path to transform your health and align with your body's natural rhythms of energy production and fat utilization. This isn't merely about adopting a diet; it's about embracing a lifestyle that reverberates through every aspect of your well-being.

Your courage to embrace this change, your curiosity to explore the unfamiliar, and your commitment to your health are what will propel you forward. The keto journey is one of discovery, learning to listen to your body, and nurturing it with the foods it was designed to thrive on. This lifestyle is a powerful tool, capable of igniting a profound transformation within, leading to enhanced vitality, improved metabolic health, and a clearer, more vibrant mental state.

Remember, the journey doesn't end here. Each day is an opportunity to deepen your understanding, refine your choices, and celebrate your successes, no matter how small. Your path to health and wellness is uniquely yours, shaped by your experiences, challenges, and triumphs.

Stay open to the endless possibilities that this lifestyle offers. Let your curiosity guide you through the nuances of keto living, from experimenting with new recipes to finding joy in the foods that fuel your body optimally. Embrace this journey with an open heart and a spirit of adventure.

Above all, know that you are supported. This book, though just one piece of your journey, is a companion in your quest for a healthier, more fulfilled life. The principles and practices shared here are designed to accompany you, offering guidance, inspiration, and encouragement as you navigate the path ahead.

So, with gratitude for the steps you've already taken and anticipation for those yet to come, we invite you to continue on this transformative journey. Your commitment to this lifestyle is a commitment to yourself, a testament to your strength and resilience. The future is bright, and it's yours for the taking. Embrace it with all the passion, determination, and grace you possess.

Thank you for embracing this journey, for every step you've taken, and for considering sharing your thoughts with others. Your support is immensely appreciated and goes far beyond the pages of this book. Together, let's continue spreading the word, inspiring change, and fostering a community of health and well-being.

I would be deeply grateful if you could share your experience and leave a positive review on Amazon.

It would not only warm my heart but also help guide others to this same path of discovery and wellness. Your words can light the way for someone else searching for a change, offering them the same hope and guidance you found within these pages.

Copyright © by TIANA BLAKELY

Made in the USA
Columbia, SC
03 July 2025

60320659R00063